Series Editor: Catherine Bowness

CW00493498

The
Faith in
Action
Series

Someone to Talk To

The Story of Chad Varah and
The Samaritans

Audrey Constant

Illustrated by Brian Platt

RMEP

RELIGIOUS AND MORAL EDUCATION PRESS

SOMEONE TO TALK TO

The Story of Chad Varah and The Samaritans

O n the day of the funeral it was pouring with rain. There were only a few people present: the men who carried the coffin, a young priest and one or two others. Inside the coffin was the body of a thirteen-year-old girl.

The name of the priest was Chad Varah. As Chad walked beside the coffin, he learned why this young girl had died. She had not been ill. Fear had driven her to despair. When she had her first monthly period, she thought the blood meant she had some dreadful disease. Because there was no one she felt she could talk to, she did not tell anyone about her secret. In the end she could bear it no longer, so she killed herself.

Since the girl had no one to talk to, there was no way she could find out what was happening to her. It was just a normal part of growing up, but to the girl it had become a terrifying experience.

The young priest was shocked at the waste of such a young life. If only the girl had been able to talk to someone – even a stranger – her life could have been saved.

As Chad buried her, he made a promise. 'Little girl,' he said, 'I never knew you, but you have changed my life.' He decided to take every chance he could to talk to young people about their problems.

What Do You Think?

Important: In answering 'What Do You Think?' questions in this book, it is important that you not only state your opinion but also give as many reasons as possible for your opinion.

1. What had frightened the young girl? If she had found someone to talk to, how might they have helped her?

2. Why is it important for most people to have someone to talk to?

3. Is it always easy to listen when someone wants to share their problems? Try to suggest some reasons why it might help young people if they were taught listening skills in school.

His Early Life

Chad Varah was born in 1911 and brought up in a Christian home, the eldest of a large family. His father was a clergyman and he wanted Chad to become a priest too. But while Chad was growing up, although he often went to church, he was not sure what he believed.

He liked science at school and was good at it. He carried on his studies at university, but when he graduated, he still had no idea what he wanted to do with his life.

For a while Chad helped in a home for handicapped children. He did the washing up and played with the children. Later on he worked for a firm that made bricks, doing chemical research. At the same time he earned extra money by writing articles for newspapers.

About this time, Chad went to see an uncle of his who had been a missionary in Africa. Chad enjoyed talking to him, even though his uncle was much older than he was. Chad called him his *guru*, which is an Indian word for 'teacher'. He discussed his future with his uncle.

'Why don't you become a priest?' asked his uncle. 'After all, you don't have a better idea, do you?'

By now God meant very much more to Chad. He went to a college in Lincoln and trained for the priesthood. He was taught by Michael Ramsay, who later became Archbishop of Canterbury. It was he who helped Chad to see that God wanted him to be a priest.

What Do You Think?

1. Some young people choose to follow the same career as their parents but others make a huge effort to do something different. How much influence should an older member of the family have on a young person's future working life?

2. Think about the people who are closest to you. Which person has had the most influence on your life so far? What situations can you think of where you might need to ask them for advice?

The Youth Club

Two years later, in 1935, Chad finished his training and went to St Giles' Church in Lincoln. There, among other things, he ran a youth club. He spent hours talking to the youngsters at the coffee bar and playing table tennis with them. To begin with they boasted about all the trouble they got into and tried out their bad language on him.

Far from shocking him, they found Chad wanted to listen and was interested in what they had to say. Their swearing did not seem to upset him at all. They agreed that, on the whole, Chad was quite a likeable fellow. Soon they came to him, one by one, and told him about their problems. They were surprised at how understanding he was.

Chad also gave sex-education classes to engaged couples. He worked with a very wise priest, the vicar of the parish, who helped him, even though some of the parishioners did not like what Chad was doing. They told him, 'Vicar, you ought to stop that young priest giving those talks to our young people.'

The vicar replied, 'My guess is that one day similar talks will be given in every church in the country.' He knew how important Chad's classes were to those couples, and how natural and beautiful Chad made sex sound.

Soon not only young people from his own church came to hear him, but also others from nearby churches.

What Do You Think?

1. Why do some young people boast about getting into trouble?

2. Why do you think the young people were surprised that swearing did not shock Chad? Do you think that this made them stop using bad language when Chad was near or would they have tried to make their language even more shocking? Give reasons for your answer.

3. Why do you think some people objected to the sex-education talks which Chad offered to engaged couples?

Children's Comics

From St Giles', Chad was sent to other churches. He was always more interested in working among young people than in doing any other kind of church work.

Towards the end of the Second World War, he went to St Paul's Church, Clapham Junction, in South London. He was also the visiting priest at St John's Hospital, Battersea. While he was there he met a clergyman friend of his called Marcus Morris. Morris was starting a children's comic called *Eagle*. It had plenty of picture stories and articles about famous people, as well as puzzles. Before long, *Eagle* was being read by children all over the country.

Morris asked Chad to help him with this comic. As he was good at science, one of Chad's jobs was to see that Dan Dare, the space hero, did not do anything that was scientifically impossible. For instance, he could not travel faster than the speed of light.

Another job Chad was given was to write the back-page story about the life of St Paul. Going home on the bus one day, he read the story of Paul in the Bible. A strange thing happened. Every scene in the story sprang to life as though he were there himself. When he arrived home he got out a piece of paper; on one side he wrote the words of the story, and on the other, ideas for pictures for the artist to follow.

There are very few people who can see scenes so clearly in their minds. They are called 'visualizers'. Morris was very pleased to find that Chad had this gift, and he kept him busy thinking up pictures for stories. *Eagle* was so successful that it was soon followed by other comics, like *Girl*, *Swift* and *Robin*.

For twelve years Chad went on working for the Church and writing for children's comics. At the same time he wrote articles for newspapers about other things that concerned him deeply.

Chad knew that many people live with secret fears, or struggle to cope with some kind of behaviour of which they are ashamed. They are often too embarrassed to discuss their problem, or to seek expert help. Chad wrote about such problems in a very helpful and sympathetic way.

Many of these articles were read by people with similar troubles. It set their minds at rest to know that they were not alone, and that other people suffered in the same way as they did. Chad did not criticize them, but was understanding and helpful. They wrote to or telephoned him, asking for advice with their own problems.

Some people, he discovered, were so worried that they did not want to go on living. In what little time he had, he tried to help them by talking to them over the telephone or replying to their letters. Some needed more time, and these he invited to come and see him.

Chad was happiest when meeting people one at a time in a sickroom, a hospital, or a prison cell. He found he was able to help them. He wanted to give all his time to this sort of work.

Chad felt that God was guiding him in this direction. He had an idea that God has a special way of making people do things: he does not shout instructions through a heavenly loudspeaker; instead, he makes all people especially good at something, then guides them to use these gifts. In other words, God's call is a challenge to people to find out what they are here *for*.

Chad felt that at last he knew what *he* was here for. He read that there were three suicides every day in Greater London. To him these were not simply numbers. They were people he could imagine dying miserably in lonely rooms, with some secret fear or a broken heart. Life had become so hard for them that they could no longer bear it. He was determined to try to help them, if they wanted to be helped. If not, he knew he had no right to interfere.

But how was he to get in touch with these people? And how would they find him? The quickest way would be by telephone. Even those who did not have their own phone could use a telephone-box. This way they could remain unseen and unknown if they wanted to.

But how could Chad do this and run his church at the same time? It seemed an impossible task. He had a talk with God. 'There must be someone else,' he argued. 'I'm busy. I have a church to run and my hospital work to do. I have my writing and a wife and four children to keep.'

What he really needed was a church without too many parishioners to care for. Then he would have more time.

What Do You Think?

1. Chad worked hard as a member of a team producing comics. Many children and young people read comics in the 1940s and 1950s. If a modern priest wanted to reach out to young people, what other methods of communication should he or she think about using today? Give reasons to support your suggestions.

2. How do comics and glossy magazines help ordinary people to cope with some of their problems?

3. Chad believed that he had no right to interfere in people's lives if they did not want him to help them. Should people be left alone with their problems if they decide that they do not want to be helped? Give reasons.

A Small Miracle

There are some London churches that are well endowed. This means that at some time in the past rich people left them enough money to pay for the running of the church and to pay the clergy who served there. The Church of St Stephen, Walbrook, is one such church. In 1953 Chad was invited to be the Rector of St Stephen's. ('Rector' is a title used in some parishes instead of 'Vicar'.)

St Stephen's is the parish church of the Lord Mayor of London. It is next door to the Mansion House, the official home of the Lord Mayor. The church was built by the great architect Sir Christopher Wren. Badly bombed during the war, it was later restored.

Luckily for Chad, St Stephen's had only a few parishioners. This was because few people actually live in the City of London, although over a million people work there during the day.

Chad accepted the job. He decided to set up his telephone service in a small room in the church.

In October 1953 he rang the Telephone Exchange Supervisor to discuss choosing a suitable telephone number for the service. In those days not many people had telephones and you could sometimes choose your own number.

Chad wanted a number that was easy to remember, like the 999 emergency number of the police, fire and ambulance services.

'How about something simple, like Mansion House 9000?' he asked the supervisor. 'But I suppose someone has that number already.'

'I expect so,' she agreed. 'What is your number at the moment?'

Chad dusted off the dial of the telephone in the shabby little room.

'It's all right!' he cried. 'It's Mansion House 9000!'

So, with this small miracle, in the midst of the rubble left by the war, he began his work of caring for people with fears and problems.

What Do You Think?

1. Why was it important for the phone number to be one which could be easily remembered?

Why 'The Samaritans'?

At last Chad had a base to operate from and an income to live on while he worked. And he had a telephone. Now he needed a name for his project.

He thought of the story of the Good Samaritan in the Bible, about a man who lay wounded and dying on a dusty road in Israel/Palestine. Everyone passed him by. They did not want to have anything to do with him. They did not want to get involved. Then the Samaritan arrived. Although he was a stranger in those parts (and a traditional enemy of the injured Jewish man), he did not hesitate. He went across to the man, gave him water and bound up his wounds. Then he put him on his donkey and took him to the nearest inn, where they looked after him.

Like the Samaritan, Chad wanted to help people who had no one else to turn to. Inspired by the story, he decided to call his organization 'The Samaritans'.

What Do You Think?

1. What aspect of the story of the Good Samaritan do you think most inspired Chad to call his group 'The Samaritans'? If you were setting up an action group to help people in difficult times, what might you call your group and why would you give it this name?

In Need of a Friend

The calls came from people of all ages and with every kind of problem. Most of them were ordinary people who had come to a crisis in their lives. Some of them had been driven to despair; others were almost ready to kill themselves. Many of them were having difficulties with their marriages. Others had lost someone they loved or depended on. There were people with drink problems. A few were mentally ill and needed expert help.

Chad listened to them all. After speaking to them over the telephone he found that many of them wanted to come and see him personally. He could not always given them enough help with just one telephone call.

Chad worked the whole day through. Sometimes he had eleven one-hour interviews in a day. Often he had to stop an interview to answer a telephone call. He did not even have time for meals. Although he had a secretary to deal with the business side of things, he was the only one who could advise these people. As a clergyman he was used to giving advice.

Just when he was wondering how he was going to manage if things went on like this, he received offers of help. These volunteers were ordinary people who did not have any special training, but who had heard of Chad's work and how busy he was. They wanted to use what time they had to help him. Some were housewives who had some spare time during the day when their children were at school. Others only had time in the evenings after work.

Chad did not immediately see how he could use these kind people, but he did not want to turn them away. Perhaps they could look after the callers while they waited to see him.

It was the volunteers, not Chad, who discovered how they could help. They turned up regularly; they made coffee and talked kindly to these people, making them feel relaxed and comfortable. And often, as they had more time than Chad did, they made a better job of comforting the callers than he could have done. Some of them went away feeling happier without even seeing Chad. The volunteers had given them the help and comfort they needed.

It didn't take Chad long to realize that what these unhappy people needed was a friend, not expert advice. They wanted someone to listen to their troubles and care about them until their difficult time was over.

Chad knew that volunteers would have to be carefully chosen and prepared for the work, but his helpers had already shown they had the qualities needed to make good Samaritans. They had offered friendship at a time of loneliness and fear.

Chad Varah at St Stephen's Church, 1965

Soon the little room where Chad had begun his telephone service became too small for him and his helpers. It was then that he discovered an old burial vault right under the church. A group of people who were interested in Chad's work paid the cost of turning the vault into rooms from which The Samaritans could operate. It was agreed that The Samaritans could always have the use of these rooms, whoever the Rector of St Stephen's might be in years to come. As time went by, more and more Samaritan centres were opened.

What Do You Think?

1. Listening to people's problems without interfering is not easy. What types of problem do you think would be the most difficult for one person alone to hear about? Why?

2. Why did Chad have difficulties when he first began his telephone service without help from others? When volunteers arrived to help him, what services did they offer which he could not provide when trying to work alone?

What Sorts of People Become Volunteers?

People from all walks of life volunteer to become Samaritans but they all have one thing in common: they want to help people in distress. Whatever their own views, one of the basic rules of The Samaritans is that volunteers should leave their personal beliefs at the door and listen to callers without prejudice on the basis of age, background, beliefs or sexual orientation.

Volunteers have to be chosen carefully, because it is not easy to help people in despair. They must be patient, ready to listen to people's troubles. They have to be able to keep to the rules they accept when they become Samaritans. They have to be reliable and not be put off by rudeness. (When people are upset they can sometimes be rude.) Chad said, 'We want those who really care, who can listen and who are humble enough to do anything for us.'

Volunteers are given full training over a period of months, and afterwards constant support and back-up.

What Do You Think?

1. Why do you think people volunteered to help Chad when they heard about his new telephone service? What qualities do you think Chad should have looked for when selecting volunteers? Why would these qualities have been important?

2. The Samaritans believe that it is important for volunteers to be specially trained. What training do you feel would be necessary for their work?

3. If you were a volunteer working to help others would you feel more confident if you knew that there was a support system behind you? Give reasons.

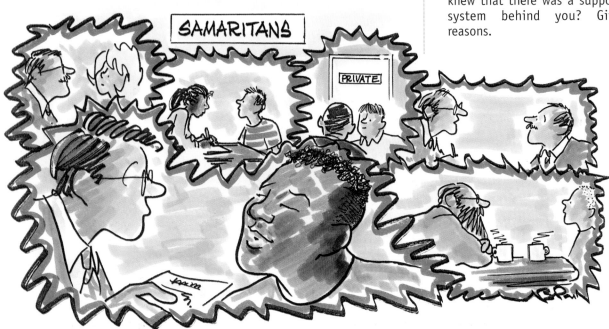

A Samaritan Centre at Work

The size of a branch and the number of volunteers staffing it varies according to the needs of the area, but overall in the U.K. and Ireland volunteers cover about 500 telephone helplines for 24 hours a day, 7 days a week, throughout the year.

A branch is run by a director and deputies, and most branches also have a secretary, a treasurer and a training officer. When expert help is required, The Samaritans can call on emergency services or other professionals or accompany callers to hospital, but *only* if requested to by the caller. All decisions about their own life are made by the caller at all times. Nothing that a Samaritan volunteer is told will be passed on, so callers need not fear that their secrets will be made known.

Sometimes The Samaritans receive a call from someone phoning on behalf of a friend or relative. 'My neighbour is very depressed. Please come and help her,' they may say. There is a rule about this. The Samaritans believe that everyone should be in charge of their own lives. Unless the call concerns a very young or very old person, or someone who is unable to help themselves, they will not go to them. Instead, they ask the caller to try to persuade that person to telephone The Samaritans themselves, and then they will try to help them.

What Do You Think?

1. What three rules kept at a Samaritan centre can you find in this section? Which of these rules do you feel is the most important (a) for the caller, (b) for the Samaritan volunteer? Which do you think is the most difficult for volunteers to keep? Explain why.

What Sorts of People Call The Samaritans?

Calls come from ordinary people of all ages who have come to a crisis in their lives. These people are often lonely because their problem separates them from the rest of the world.

Not everyone has friends and relatives they can talk to when they are troubled. Perhaps the callers' problems are too personal to tell other people about anyway. They might even want to talk *about* their friends or family.

The Samaritans do not only help adults. Many of their callers are under 25 and some of them are schoolchildren. Nor is the organization only for people who are really desperate or want to harm themselves. Nevertheless, more and more desperate young people are calling The Samaritans.

The 'case histories' on the brown panels below and opposite may help to show why people contact The Samaritans. **They are not true stories**, because The Samaritans always help in confidence and never tell anyone else what their callers have told them.

However these 'case histories' give examples of the kinds of problem that arise and how they might be dealt with.

Jane had been going out with Don ever since she left school. Everyone knew that he was her boyfriend. Although it had never actually been mentioned, Jane felt that it was only a matter of time before they married. Then one day Jane's cousin, Carol, came to work in the same town. Carol stayed with Jane's family while she looked for somewhere else to live. At first Jane was glad to have Carol. She was fun to be with and she was pretty. Don thought so too. Although she didn't want to believe it, Jane noticed that Don was soon paying Carol more attention than herself.

Jane hoped that when Carol found a place to live, Don would see less of her and forget her, but it didn't happen that way. It was Jane who saw less of Don and she knew that Carol was taking her place with him.

Jane felt let down and miserable. She did not want to go out with her friends. They all knew about her and Don and she couldn't face them. She could not expect any sympathy from Mum and Dad either. They had never liked Don much. She was desperate.

Then she saw a notice about The Samaritans. She picked up the phone and soon she was telling someone called Eileen all about it. Eileen invited her to the centre. Over a cup of tea, Jane began to feel better. Here was someone who really understood how she felt. Although it did not bring Don back, life somehow didn't look quite so bleak any more.

Martin lived with his mother and stepfather, but it was not a happy home. His stepfather never liked him and often lost his temper. Martin did not spend longer than he had to at home. Whenever he could he went out with his friends.

There had been times when they had been in trouble, and although Martin was ready to take a few risks, he didn't like the sorts of thing they had been up to lately. He didn't want to be accused of chickening out, though. He would lose what friends he had and life would be even lonelier.

One day the gang broke into a shop. Martin hadn't actually gone in, but the police rightly guessed he was one of them. He was let off with a warning. That really frightened him. Where was all this going to lead? He didn't want this sort of life but if he stayed at home, his stepfather would go on at him, and he couldn't stand that. Life was simply not worth living.

He didn't know anything about The Samaritans, but he had seen one of their notices somewhere. Probably they could do nothing for him, he thought, but he was desperate enough to try them. It was quite late at night when he rang. The man's voice at the other end of the line was reassuring. In fact, the centre was not far away, so Martin went round for a chat.

After that he called in quite often and talked to Frank. Gradually, with Frank's help, he gained confidence and began to think about what he really wanted to do with his life.

What Do You Think?

There are particular difficulties about being young – finding friends, discovering about sex, coping at school or with parents at home, becoming independent. Problems always seem worse when you try to bottle them up.

In the end, some people attempt suicide. Few really want to die. They just do not want to live with things as they are.

1. It is claimed that although some people attempt suicide, few people really want to die. Why do you think someone who doesn't really want to die might attempt suicide?

What Happens When a Caller Rings?

When the phone rings in a Samaritan centre, the volunteer on duty answers with the words, 'The Samaritans – can I help you?' Those six words are very important. From the sound of the voice, the caller decides whether they can talk to that person about their problem. If they can't, they may put the phone down and try to struggle on alone, or they may wait a while and then ring again. This time perhaps a different voice answers. The caller begins to talk.

It may take a long time. The caller does not know where to begin. They may talk about all sorts of other things before they feel they can trust the volunteer enough to tell them the real cause of their despair.

The caller can talk for as long as they like. They do not have to give their name if they don't want to. The volunteer tries to make them feel at ease, reassuring them that no one else will know about the conversation. Often there is no easy answer to the problem. But the volunteer will not tell the caller what to do. They will try to help the caller to calm down, giving them time and space to explore their feelings. This can be the first step towards finding a way forward so that the caller can, in time, make up their own mind.

Volunteers might never find out what happens to callers with whom they have talked for hours. Sometimes they have no idea whether they were able to help at all. It is enough that they were there to offer warmth and friendship at a time of need.

What Do You Think?

1. A Samaritan who takes a call may never know what happens to the caller. Give examples to show when this may make their work (a) easier, (b) more difficult.

A Samaritan talks about their experience of becoming and working as a volunteer

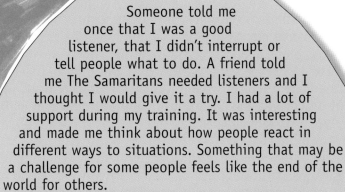

Someone told me once that I was a good listener, that I didn't interrupt or tell people what to do. A friend told me The Samaritans needed listeners and I thought I would give it a try. I had a lot of support during my training. It was interesting and made me think about how people react in different ways to situations. Something that may be a challenge for some people feels like the end of the world for others.

You must have seen our adverts in papers, on bookmarks, on notice-boards and in toilets. Everyone knows about The Samaritans, the group which gives telephone support to suicidal people, but most of the callers on my phone are not about to kill themselves. They are simply people who need a listener, someone who will not judge them or give them a lecture but a person who will allow them space to speak. Sometimes as they speak I can almost hear them making a decision for themselves.

I don't tell people what to do. I don't know if I have helped anyone. I hope I have. I simply stay on the line until callers are ready to say goodbye. I'm a friend at the end of the line, a loyal friend who will never tell anyone who has been talking to me or what they have said. The Samaritans are a confidential service. I think that is why we are respected.

The Festival Branch

A crowd can be a very lonely place. At pop festivals, for example, where everyone else seems to be having fun, an unhappy person can feel very much alone.

A group of young Samaritans believed they might be able to help in this situation. They formed a team to visit pop festivals. They wanted to find out more about young people's problems by being amongst them.

Now the Festival Branch operates all over the U.K. and Ireland. Currently there are about 80 volunteers in the Branch and their numbers at any event, and their shifts, vary tremendously, but volunteers are available 24 hours a day. Most of them are already serving in town branches of The Samaritans or similar organizations. Often they have to work in noisy, crowded, tense conditions, so most (but not all) of the volunteers are young. When they are off duty the volunteers mingle with the crowds and enjoy the festival like everyone else.

What Do You Think?

1. Why can a person sometimes be lonely even when surrounded by people? If you wish, give an example of an occasion when you felt miserable when others seemed to be happy.

Looking Ahead

These days there are over two hundred Samaritan centres in the U.K. and the Republic of Ireland and nearly 20 000 volunteers. They take over 4½ million calls a year and can now be reached by phone, by textphone (for the deaf and hard of hearing), face to face at branches, by letter and by e-mail. Samaritan-style organizations now operate in over forty countries under the umbrella of an organization called Befrienders International.

Calls to The Samaritans have doubled in ten years and the number of e-mails has more than tripled in the last three years. The Samaritans work in partnership with local and national Government as well as with the media, to make more people aware of suicide.

The Samaritan branches also work with their local communities in reaching out to schools, hospitals and people on the streets to encourage them to share their time and skills with people at risk from suicide or self-harm.

Their training resources are also used by people in business firms and those working in education and health. For instance, research is being carried out among young people, focusing on issues of concern such as alcohol and drug use, bullying and self-esteem. The Samaritans have produced a Youth Pack to help teachers and pupils discuss issues like anxiety in the classroom.

In the year 2000, The Samaritans ran a special Valentine's Day campaign that encouraged young people who were worried about their relationships to talk to a friend or to a Samaritan.

It is not always easy to tell when young people are desperately worried or upset about something. Sometimes they can't talk about it or feel that people might not want to listen. The Samaritans want to encourage everyone to look out for those around them and to take time to listen and support them, as this can be crucial in helping them to get through a crisis.

The Samaritans also work in prisons, providing support for prisoners. They are also concerned about people living in rural areas such as farmers who, in these difficult times, are at risk through isolation and stress.

The Samaritans continually work to create new links with other groups and they are expanding their training expertise for use by other organizations.

In September 2000, HRH the Prince of Wales took over from the Duchess of Kent as Patron of The Samaritans.

Fund-Raising

The Samaritans are run by volunteers, with only a small team of paid administration staff. Nevertheless, it costs £2.10 on average to answer each of the 4½ million calls each year from people in need of their support. They are funded by several big companies as well as individual supporters who commit money to The Samaritans on a regular basis. For example, in the year 2000 two substantial grants came from The National Lottery Charities Board as well as donations from other organizations and trusts. People also contributed through personal gifts of money and by purchasing Samaritans Christmas cards. Every penny The Samaritans are given is vital in keeping their service running all day, every day.

And all the time The Samaritans get busier and busier.

What Do You Think?

1. Why do you think that The Samaritans are getting busier and busier?

Biographical Notes

Chad Varah was born on 12 November 1911, the eldest son of the Vicar of Barton-on-Humber, Humberside.

He was educated at Worksop College, Nottinghamshire, and later obtained a scholarship to Keble College, Oxford, where he studied Natural Sciences. After his graduation, in 1933 he trained for the priesthood at Lincoln Theological College.

Between 1935 and 1942 Chad Varah worked as a curate (assistant priest) in churches in Lincoln, London and Barrow-in-Furness. He was appointed Vicar of Holy Trinity Church, Blackburn, in 1942. In 1949 he became Vicar of St Paul's Church, Clapham Junction, in London. In 1953 he became Rector of the Church of St Stephen, Walbrook, in the City of London, the parish church of the Lord Mayor of London.

From 1950 to 1961 Chad Varah worked as Scriptwriter and Visualizer for *Eagle* and *Girl* comics as well as carrying out his church duties.

In 1953 he founded The Samaritans, an organization to help the despairing and suicidal. The first branch of The Samaritans was set up at St Stephen's, in the City of London. There are now over 200 branches of The Samaritans in the United Kingdom and the Republic of Ireland, dealing with more than 4½ million telephone calls a year.

Chad Varah was the Director of the London branch of The Samaritans until 1974, when he became its President.

Chad Varah's awards and honours include the O.B.E. (Officer of the Order of the British Empire), the Albert Schweitzer Gold Medal, the Prix de l'Institut de la Vie and the Roumanian Patriarchal Cross. He has also been awarded an Honorary Doctorate by Leicester University and is an Honorary Fellow at Keble College, Oxford.

Things to Do

1 Imagine that you are applying to a grant-awarding organization for money to set up a branch of The Samaritans or similar group in your own area. Write a brief outline of the aims of your group and show how you would put a grant to good use.

2 Imagine that a person is feeling very lonely and miserable after **either** finishing with their partner **or** the death of a much-loved pet. Using pages 13 and 16 to help you, write an imaginary script of a conversation between that person and a Samaritan volunteer.

3 Imagine a person who has been helped by The Samaritans when he or she was in despair. Write a letter from that person to a Samaritan centre thanking them for the help they gave.

4 Design a poster or a web page showing the work of The Samaritans and encouraging people to become volunteers.

5 Design a bookmark which could be left in a local library showing how The Samaritans can offer help when someone wants to talk about their problems.

6 Make a list of all the places where you think information about The Samaritans could and should be left or displayed. Give a brief reason why each place is important.

7 When Chad first set up The Samaritans the telephone was the quickest method of communication. What other quick methods could be used today? Describe how some of these might be used and show how you think they might alter the work of The Samaritans.

8 Look at a map of your local area and in groups decide where the best place for a Samaritan centre would be.

9 Imagine that you are in charge of a new Samaritan centre and that you are going to interview some would-be volunteers. In small groups produce a list of suitable questions to ask or tasks which you might ask the interviewees to do.

10 Design and present your own plans for an ideal Samaritan centre. Think about the space, types of area and equipment that you would need to run the centre according to the rules about privacy.

11 Make (a) a list of all the qualities you have which would make you a good Samaritan volunteer and (b) a list of the things you might find difficult.

Questions for Assessment or Examination Candidates

12 (a) Explain why and how the story of the Good Samaritan inspired Chad Varah. (5 marks)

(b) State the qualities a Samaritan volunteer should have and give reasons why these are important. (5 marks)

(c) Explain two of the most important rules for Samaritan volunteers. (10 marks)

13 (a) Years ago it was a crime to attempt suicide and survivors of failed suicide attempts could be sent to prison. Why did some religious believers think that to take one's life was a sin and why did others believe that those who tried to die were simply asking for help? (10 marks)

(b) If a religious believer from a religion you have studied was a Samaritan volunteer, which rules from their religion would they be following? (5 marks)

(c) 'If people have problems they should pull themselves together and get on with life rather than expecting others to help them for nothing!'

How might a Samaritan volunteer argue against this point of view? (5 marks)

Religious and Moral Education Press
*A division of SCM-Canterbury Press Ltd,
a wholly owned subsidiary of
Hymns Ancient & Modern Ltd
St Mary's Works, St Mary's Plain
Norwich, Norfolk NR3 3BH*

Story copyright © 1981, 2002
Audrey Constant

Questions copyright © 2002
Catherine Bowness

Audrey Constant has asserted her right
under the Copyright, Designs and
Patents Act, 1988, to be identified as
Author of this Work.

*All rights reserved. No part of this
publication may be reproduced, stored in
a retrieval system, or transmitted, in any
form or by any means, electronic,
electrostatic, magnetic tape, mechanical,
photocopying, recording or otherwise,
without permission in writing from the
publishers.*

First published 1981

New edition first published 2002

ISBN 1 85175 262 5

Designed and typeset by
TOPICS – The Creative Partnership,
Exeter

Printed in Great Britain by
Format Print and Design, Middlefield
Industrial Estate, Sandy, Bedfordshire
for SCM-Canterbury Press Ltd, Norwich

Notes for Teachers

The first Faith in Action books were published in the late 1970s and the series has remained popular with both teachers and pupils. However, much in education has changed over the last twenty years, such as the development of both new examination syllabuses in Religious Studies and local agreed syllabuses for Religious Education which place more emphasis on pupils' own understanding, interpretation and evaluation of religious belief and practice, rather than a simple knowledge of events. This has encouraged us to amend the style of the Faith in Action Series to make it more suitable for today's classroom.

The aim is, as before, to tell the stories of people who have lived and acted according to their faith, but we have included alongside the main story questions which will encourage pupils to think about the reasons for the behaviour of our main characters and to empathize with the situations in which they found themselves. We hope that pupils will also be able to relate some of the issues in the stories to other issues in modern society, either in their own area or on a global scale.

The 'What Do You Think?' questions may be used for group or class discussion or for short written exercises. The 'Things to Do' at the end of the story include ideas for longer activities and more-structured questions suitable for assessment or examination practice.

In line with current syllabus requirements, as Britain is a multifaith society, Faith in Action characters will be selected from a wide variety of faith backgrounds and many of the questions may be answered from the perspective of more than one faith.

CMB, 1997

Acknowledgements
Photographs are reproduced by kind permission of Hart Associates Ltd.